W9-AUD-027

DISCOVERING AMERICA
★ An Exceptional Nation ★

American Geography
and the Environment

Cassandra Schumacher

Cavendish
Square

New York

Published in 2019 by Cavendish Square Publishing, LLC
243 5th Avenue, Suite 136, New York, NY 10016

Copyright © 2019 by Cavendish Square Publishing, LLC

First Edition

No part of this publication may be reproduced, stored in a retrieval system, or transmitted in any form or by any means—electronic, mechanical, photocopying, recording, or otherwise—without the prior permission of the copyright owner. Request for permission should be addressed to Permissions, Cavendish Square Publishing, 243 5th Avenue, Suite 136, New York, NY 10016. Tel (877) 980-4450; fax (877) 980-4454.

Website: cavendishsq.com

This publication represents the opinions and views of the author based on his or her personal experience, knowledge, and research. The information in this book serves as a general guide only. The author and publisher have used their best efforts in preparing this book and disclaim liability rising directly or indirectly from the use and application of this book.

All websites were available and accurate when this book was sent to press.

Library of Congress Cataloging-in-Publication Data

Names: Schumacher, Cassandra, author.
Title: American geography and the environment / Cassandra Schumacher.
Description: First edition. | New York : Cavendish Square, 2019. | Series: Discovering America: an exceptional nation | Includes bibliographical references and index.
Identifiers: LCCN 2018030831 (print) | LCCN 2018031063 (ebook) | ISBN 9781502643124 (ebook) | ISBN 9781502642660 (library bound) | ISBN 9781502643117 (pbk.)
Subjects: LCSH: United States--Historical geography. | Environmental geography--United States.
Classification: LCC E179.5 (ebook) | LCC E179.5 .S365 2019 (print) | DDC 911/.73--dc23
LC record available at https://lccn.loc.gov/2018030831

Editorial Director: David McNamara
Editor: Caitlyn Miller
Copy Editor: Rebecca Rohan
Associate Art Director: Alan Sliwinski
Designer: Joe Parenteau
Production Coordinator: Karol Szymczuk
Photo Research: J8 Media

The photographs in this book are used by permission and through the courtesy of: Cover Welcomia/Shutterstock.com; p. 4 Erik Harrison/Shutterstock.com; p. 7 North Wind Picture Archives; p. 9 Vladislav Gajic/Shutterstock.com; p. 11 Universal History Archive/UIG/Getty Images; p. 14-15 (used throughout) tgavrano/Shutterstock.com; p. 27 Paul Revere Boston/Wikimedia Commons/File:Boston Massacre highres.Jpg/Public Domain; p. 31 Victorian Traditions/Shutterstock.com; p. 36 Phillip Augustavo/Alamy Stock Photo; p. 38 Jose Gil/Shutterstock.com; p. 40, 67, 75 Everett Historical/Shutterstock.com; p. 45 Graphica Artis /Bridgeman Images; p. 46-47 Courtesy of the University of Texas Libraries, The University of Texas at Austin/Wikimedia Commons/File:Oregontrail 1907.jpg/CC BY SA; p.49 Thomas R Machnitzki/Wikimedia Commons/File:Village Creek State Park Wynne AR 52.jpg/CC BY SA 3.0; p. 51 Universal History Archive/UIG/Getty Images; p. 56 GraphicaArtis/Getty Images; p. 62-63 Library of Congress/Wikimedia Commons/File:New York City, 1900 LCCN2007661108.tif/Public Domain; p. 65 Library of Congress; p. 71 PhotoQuest/Getty Images; p. 73 American Stock/Getty Images; p. 78 George Rinhart/Corbis via Getty Images; p. 80 Ullstein Bild/Getty Images; p. 83 Hulton Archive/Getty Images; p. 85 Bill Chaplis/AP Images; p. 87 Bettmann/Getty Images; p. 91 Corbac40/Shutterstock.com; p. 97 Patrick Tr/Shutterstock.com.

Printed in the United States of America

★ CONTENTS ★

The Grand Canyon is an incredible natural phenomenon that was created by millions of years of erosion.

Chapter One

Seeds of a Nation: 1491–1800

★ ★ ★ ★ ★ ★ ★

From the Eastern Seaboard to the West Coast, America has a diverse landscape featuring mountains and open plains; large, robust cities; and truly astounding natural formations. Natural wonders like the Grand Canyon and Niagara Falls and man-made features like the Hoover Dam and the Golden Gate Bridge dot the country. A combination of human creation and natural evolution, the American landscape is singular. The nation's geography bears the marks of more than two hundred years of history and demonstrates both the power of nature and humankind's ingenuity. The land and environment of America directly impacted the country's development and history, and it

★ ★ ★ ★ ★ ★ ★

continues to affect contemporary life and politics today. While much has changed in the United States of America in the five centuries since Christopher Columbus first arrived on American shores, the land remains a defining aspect, worn by time and altered forever by human use.

The history of the United States, however, reaches much farther back than early European contact—about fifteen thousand years prior to European contact, in fact. The history of the land that became the United States starts with Native peoples. Thousands of years before Columbus even imagined crossing the Atlantic to seek treasure and wealth, Native Americans roamed the lands. Indigenous people navigated the rivers and the lakes, made use of the flora and fauna, waged war, and found peace. Rich societies developed, shaped around the abundant resources the lands and waters had to offer. These communities did not look like those of feudal Europe, which Columbus and his contemporaries saw as "civilized." However, there is no denying that at the time of Columbus's first contact, Native Americans had complex and rich societies that made use of their environment and its resources in sophisticated ways. America's history long predates the written historical record. Though dependent on an oral history rather than a written one, Native Americans called America their home for thousands of years and therefore make up an important part of its history.

Native Lands and Cultures

The resources in America vary greatly by region, each with a distinct climate. The United States is a country that contains deciduous forests and plains as well as mountain ranges and deserts. Native American societies were well adapted to those variances, and different Native tribes used different societal structures to fit the demands of their chosen climates. Their societies were shaped by their geographic location.

For example, in the Northeast, tribes occupied the region between the Atlantic Ocean and the Mississippi River. It is a temperate region with many deciduous and taiga forests as well as wetlands, waterways, and coasts. Summers and winters are cold. This region was occupied by the Algonquian and the Haudenosaunee people. These

Haudenosaunee families lived in longhouses with their maternal relatives.

tribes were known for cultivating native plants like maize, beans, and squash, as well as hunting deer and waterfowl and gathering seeds, berries, nuts, and maple syrup. They fished the waters of the region as well.

The Haudenosaunee (also known as the Iroquois) were called "the people of the longhouse," in honor of their impressive longhouses crafted out of wood, branches, and bark. These homes were designed to protect inhabitants, even in colder months. The family unit that lived in the longhouse consisted of the nuclear family of parents and children as well as the grandparents, aunts, uncles, and their children from the mother's side of the family.

The Southeastern tribes had different needs. Living along the Eastern Seaboard and down the Gulf Coast were the Cherokee, the Choctaw, the Chickasaw, the Creek, and the Seminole tribes. These tribes tended to establish their communities around the waterways in the area and were hunter-gatherers as well as fishermen. Their territory extended through what is today Texas, Oklahoma, Arkansas, Missouri, Kentucky, the Virginias, North Carolina, and Maryland. They built large farming communities that are considered America's earliest cities. Historians believe that Cahokia, which was built in modern Illinois, sustained a population of up to twenty thousand people and spanned about 4,000 acres (1,619 hectares). The farming fields of Cahokia were near large, human-built mounds.

In Cahokia, large earthen mounds were constructed to serve as burial sites and monuments and for ceremonial purposes.

Past the Mississippi were the tribes of the Great Plains. Their territories went as far as the Rocky Mountains. These tribes include the Cheyenne, the Mandan, the Sioux, and Pawnee people as well as the Osage Nation, among many others. The plains were dry and open lands, with sprawling fields protected by high grasses. Large herds of big game like bison roamed freely. Adapting to that environment, the Native Americans of the plains were nomadic and lived in transportable tepees. Tepees are tall, cone-shaped structures made of small, thin strips of wood and animal skins. Because they were easy to to pack and move, tepees were well suited to the tribes' hunting and gathering lifestyles. The communities moved frequently to follow herds of bison and gather food.

The Great Basin was also populated by many different tribes, who spoke many different languages. Much like the plains, the Great Basin was characterized by hunting and gathering societies. Located in what is today Nevada and Utah as well as parts of Oregon, Idaho, California, and other nearby states, the Great Basin is bordered by three mountain ranges: the Wasatch Mountains, the Sierra Nevada Mountains, and the Cascade Mountains. It features a dry, desert landscape because the mountains block the heavy rains of the northern West Coast. Native people adapted to the arid climate by hunting game like antelope and jackrabbits and harvesting tubers from the dry ground. Some tribes were able to farm and fish if they were near enough to water, but hunting animals like deer, elk, and mountain sheep was more common. The tribes also crafted elaborately decorated baskets and pottery to gather foraged berries and roots. While the Great Basin was not well suited for farming because of the climate, the people who lived there knew where to look for food in their unique environment.

The lifestyles of the Southwestern tribes were also shaped by their environment, though they left hunting and gathering behind to become cultivators of local edible plants. Additionally, the tribes of the Southwest are famous

The Pueblo architecture of Adobe Village in Taos, New Mexico, was photographed in 1900.

for their architecture. The rocky, dry, and mountainous topography of the American Southwest required that Southwestern tribes like the Zuni, Apache, Navajo, Cherokee, and Chiricahua people be very innovative when constructing homes and infrastructure. They were famous for their elaborate irrigation systems that allowed them to water their crops like maize, tobacco, beans, and even cotton in spite of the arid environment they lived in. Raising crops and hunting fed their communities.

Some members of the Southwestern tribes are also known as the Pueblo peoples. ("Pueblo" means "town" in Spanish.) Pueblos' homes consisted of distinct limestone, adobe, and wood structures with flat tops and sometimes more than one level. Adobe homes consisted of clay bricks that were sealed together using more clay, which dried in the hot desert sun. The homes and towns are massive architectural feats that were modeled after the homes of the Anasazi (very early ancestors of the Southwestern Pueblo people), which were carved into the cliff of the hills and mountains using similar building materials.

Tribes that inhabited the West Coast were very different from their Southwestern counterparts. They were fishing societies. Tribes that occupied this region included, but were not limited to, the Chinookan people, the Nez Perce, the Hupa, the Yurok, the Klickitat, and the Umatilla. Their territories spanned all the way up the western coast, through Canada, and just to the edge of modern Alaska. Bound to the coasts by the thick mountain ranges that run between the Midwest and the ocean, the mountains created a barrier, trapping warmer currents and producing higher temperatures and heavy rains. Thick coniferous (cone-bearing trees like firs and spruce) forests were close to the coasts and provided flora for gathering. Seafood and gathered food were the bulk of West Coast tribes' diet.

These tribes were also famous for their social stratification, which somewhat reflected feudal Europe because people were classified by their rank. As in Europe, the people with higher rank controlled the resources and lands for a particular region. In turn, the people of lower ranks lived on the lands and received resources based on rank. It was like having a large communal home for around one hundred people. Everyone who lived in these communities were considered relatives, and those most closely related to an original founding ancestor were considered more politically powerful than those with a more distant relationship. Such social stratification was rare among Native people, who tended to have more egalitarian societies. Regardless of social structure, it is apparent that the different tribes adapted to thrive in the diverse landscape of North America.

Europeans in America

When Christopher Columbus first made contact with America in December 1492, he landed in what is today Haiti. Columbus was seeking a western route to the East Indies so that he would not need to sail around the Cape of Good Hope at the tip of the African continent. Columbus missed the mark widely and instead landed in the Caribbean on an inhabited island. There, the native Taíno people had complex societies that were believed to be at their peak at the time of first contact. Columbus failed to recognize the structure of Taíno society and assumed them to be savages. Because they did not have guns, Columbus was quick to label the Taíno as vulnerable and easy to conquer.

A Letter for a King

On his return trip to Spain—after encountering what he thought was Asia but was instead the Americas—Christopher Columbus wrote a letter to King Ferdinand of Spain, who had financed the voyage. This letter was later printed in Rome as a public pamphlet and formally presented the existence of a new continent. Columbus wrote:

> I discovered many islands inhabited by numerous people. I took possession of all of them for our most fortunate King by making public proclamation and unfurling his standard, no one making resistance.

After claiming the New World for Spain, Columbus also exalted its virtues:

> The island … as well as the others in its neighborhood, is exceedingly fertile. It has numerous harbors on all sides, very safe and wide … Through it flow many very broad and health-giving rivers; and there are numerous very lofty mountains. All these island[s] are very beautiful, and of quite different shapes; easy to be transverse, and full of the greatest variety of trees reaching to the stars.

Christopher Columbus lived from 1451 to 1506.

From there, Columbus continued by describing the farming and potential ease of trade thanks to the harbors and rivers. He mentioned there were stores of gold and silver, as well as claiming that the Native people were fearful and poorly protected because they did not have the weaponry the Spaniards did. Columbus sold the idea that the New World was the perfect place for Spain to conquer and colonize.

With a single letter, Columbus opened the New World to what would become a European invasion. He thought he had discovered a new route to Asia and instead introduced Europeans to an unknown continent. America's existence and riches were announced in Europe, and the continent would be plundered.

It was not long before Columbus created the first colonial settlement and claimed the island of Haiti for Spain. He even dubbed it "Hispaniola" in honor of Spain. Columbus, unaware that America existed, still believed he had made landfall in the East Indies. (He would eventually realize his error.) Columbus's mistake proved catastrophic for the Taíno. Within little more than ten years, the island's native inhabitants were exploited and enslaved. The Spanish took the gold from Hispaniola's mines and ravaged the island's resources. According to a case study presented by Yale University, within twenty-five years of the first contact, a population that had been estimated to be over a million people stood at a mere thirty-two thousand as a direct result of European presence. It was the beginning of a merciless and massive genocide that would ravage Native American land and indigenous societies as European colonists took over. The Columbian Exchange began, decimating indigenous societies in its wake.

The Columbian Exchange

As a direct result of Columbus's first contact with the Americas, Spain began the first wave of European colonization there. What resulted was a huge transfer of plants, animals, humans, and disease in a cross-cultural exchange that was unprecedented and has yet to be repeated to such an extreme. Known as the Columbian Exchange, this trade of ideas, goods, and resources dramatically impacted both the New World and Europe. It forever changed life on both sides of the world.

As Spain colonized Middle America, also known as Mesoamerica, the Columbian Exchange spread. The Europeans brought steel technology like plows, knives, and guns, as well as the written word. The Americas presented new crops like chilies, maize, and squashes. The potato, which is easy to grow and is a calorie-dense food, came from the Americas and almost single-handedly led a huge population boom in Europe. In fact, the New World provided a cornucopia of new foods and goods. Tobacco and cocoa were coveted cash crops, and sugar and coffee grew well in the fertile and warm climate of the Caribbean, leading to a global boost in production and consumption of both. In return, high-calorie grains like wheat came from the Old World to be grown in the Americas.

Animals were a key part of the exchange too. Domesticated animals were brought to the Americas by Europeans. Livestock like sheep, goats, cattle, pigs, and horses came over with the Europeans and found new homes in the Americas. In return, Europe received llamas and birds. However, the animals brought a terrible consequence with them: disease.

The domestication of animals has always gone hand in hand with the spread of disease. Humans can be susceptible to diseases and bacteria that animals naturally carry, and living in close quarters with animals therefore leads to increased exposure to disease. In Europe, over the generations of domestication, people had built up immunity to many of the different diseases carried by domesticated livestock, but the same was not true of the people living in the Americas. Indigenous Americans did not domesticate animals on the same scale as Europeans had, so Native peoples' immune systems were not equipped to fight the onslaught of new bacteria and disease. When Europeans arrived in America, they brought a slew of deadly diseases that completely decimated the indigenous populations. Malaria, small pox, influenza, typhoid, measles, plague, and many other diseases annihilated indigenous populations. European enslavement and atrocities against indigenous people, combined with disease, led to a massive genocide that is estimated to have killed 90 percent of the American indigenous population within one hundred years of European settlement.

The effect of disease led to further atrocities. The Spaniards began importing slaves from Africa to compensate for the declining number of indigenous people available to farm the plantations the Spanish had created. The New World had been colonized for its land and the resources it could provide, but the exploitation went much further than just land and extended to the people who already lived there. European nations jumped at the opportunity to carve up the New World into colonies that would provide new resources. The geography and tribes of the Americas were officially changed forever.

European Colonization

The sixteenth and seventeenth centuries were marked by an influx of European nations' entrance into the Americas. These countries wanted the wealth that came with colonization as well as the resources that could be found in the New World. With land came new opportunities to gather raw materials and resources. It was an opportunity to gain wealth and power. North America was being divided between European powers and used as a pawn in the game of international power and politics.

Spain began the trend in Mesoamerica by seeking gold and riches, but it also colonized the parts of southern North America that would eventually become Florida, Louisiana, and Texas.

The French were much more driven by trade. Setting up a large fur-trading enterprise down the Saint Lawrence River, French focus was fixed on the North American beaver instead of on forming permanent settlements. The pelts from animals in the northern portions of the continent were coveted for high-society fashions back in

France, and water routes into territories that would much later become Canada were valuable for the access they granted to beavers for trade. The French traded with Native Americans for beaver pelts that were shipped back home to France down the Saint Lawrence.

The Dutch, however, claimed the land along the Eastern Seaboard that is today New York State. While the French were traders, the Dutch were farmers. Starting in 1624 with a settlement on Manhattan Island, the Dutch formed New Amsterdam and set to farming the fertile region. The Dutch later formally purchased the land from the Native Americans that lived there in 1626, but conflict broke out between the two groups as the Native Americans did not fully comprehend the Dutch's intent to own and control the land. The colony, however, remained in Dutch hands until it was lost to the British in 1664.

The British crown was strongly motivated by the revenue colonies could bring in. Different regions of America provided different goods, resources, and most importantly, cash crops. Farming in the colonies made them self-sufficient for the most part, as well as financially valuable. Colonies cost very little to run but brought income and resources into the mother country. Though some of the colonies were originally founded by colonists seeking religious tolerance—like Plymouth and Pennsylvania—most of the colonies were designed for economic gain.

Northeastern colonies had thick forests for lumber and maple syrup that flourished as the weather turned colder in the fall and winter. Furs could be harvested from the wildlife that needed the pelts to stay warm in the colder climates, and coastal access in New England meant whaling, which ensured that there was oil to be sold. Middle colonies like Jamestown and Maryland had a great environment for farming tobacco, which was hugely popular in Europe, but they also contributed grains like wheat and corn. Lumber from logging, ships, coal, and textiles became popular exports from these colonies as well.

The southern colonies, however, were graced with warm weather for most of the year. This meant they had a longer growing season for cash crops. Carolina produced crops like cotton and indigo. Carolina also had rice plantations, as did Georgia. The warm weather was good for growing sugar, and tobacco could grow there as well. The expansive lands also ensured that large farming enterprises called plantations could be set up. These large-scale farms usually produced a cash crop in mass amounts and were farmed by enslaved people.

Conflict in the Valley

The only dilemma that hindered British money-making was that the lands where the colonies were established were already inhabited. Tensions grew between Native Americans and colonists as the colonies moved farther into the Ohio River Valley. Encroaching colonists displaced Native people and angered the French, who were also in the Ohio River Valley. Tempers mounted between the French and the British as more colonists moved into the area. Ultimately, war broke out over the land and raged from 1754 until 1763. Battle lines were drawn between the French and the British. Nearby Native tribes chose sides. Known as the French and Indian War (or as the Seven Years' War), the British fought to protect their colonies against the French and their Native American allies. The British triumphed and came away with French territory in Canada as well as the Spanish territory in Florida.

With British holdings in America growing substantially, it would have seemed as if the nation had come out larger and stronger for the efforts in the Ohio River Valley, but with war came debt, and Britain desperately needed more money. Waging war was expensive, and King George and Parliament felt that, as the debt had accrued as a result of American defense, the colonists could help pay for it. Taxes were voted for and set in place by Parliament. These new taxes were designed to help defray the cost of the Seven Years' War. It seemed so simple, if only the colonies had seen it that way. Had King George anticipated what those minor taxes would eventually cost him, it is hard not to wonder if his choices may have been different. While the king thought the Americans should pay, the colonists decided to rebel instead.

Roadmap to the Revolution

When Great Britain passed tax legislation on the American colonies after the Seven Years' War, those laws were designed to limit trade. Legal trade for goods in the colonies was almost entirely with Britain due to the Navigation Acts of 1651. The Navigation Acts required colonists to trade with England exclusively, which raised the cost of doing business and extended the length of the process. It made England more money, and it made the colonists angry. Smuggling and piracy became more common as a means of circumventing the British orders, but after the French and Indian War, Great Britain was heavily restricting all trading and colonial shipping. The mother country now *needed* the extra income from trade with the colonies to cover the costs of the French and Indian War. Britain began enforcing taxes on goods that Americans used widely, like paper products and tea. The new tax legislation made tension over shipping restrictions boil over.

Colonists' biggest point of contention was actually directly related to geography. Fury stemmed from the distance between the mother country and the colonies. In the hundred years since initial colonization, the American subjects to the crown started to see themselves as distant from their British counterparts. Colonies had independent governments and essentially ruled themselves by that point. Having Parliament pass legislation that regulated their trade and taxed the colonists felt alien. Americans were British subjects, but they were far removed geographically and socially from the British government. Furthermore, the colonists had no one in Parliament to vote to protect their political interests, so the British taxes, though small, were met with huge amounts of resistance.

Colonists ultimately boycotted British goods, and British merchants saw their businesses wither due to American resistance. Riots broke out on both sides of the Atlantic. The tension waxed and waned as levies were passed and rescinded in the coming years, but the colonists' anger never truly abated. Restlessness was growing, and the gap between American ideology and that of the British government grew ever wider.

As Great Britain continued to tighten restrictions on American trade and exports, the colonies, which had always seen themselves as individual and separate entities, became increasingly united. In 1773, the tension came to a head when the East India Company was granted the exclusive right to trade tea in the Americas. Bostonians rioted, and a group of liberal rebels, the Sons of Liberty, disguised themselves as Native Americans and took to the harbor in protest. They boarded East India trading vessels, cracked open the crates of tea, and dumped the taxed tea straight into the Boston Harbor. Valued at $1 million in modern currency, the tea blackened the waters and British goodwill.

Parliament passed the Coercive Acts in the spring of 1774 in retribution, and the colonies went wild. The laws closed the Boston port, essentially cutting off Massachusetts's economy, which depended on trade by sea, shipping and ship making, and whaling. The Coercive Acts also dissolved Massachusetts's local government and included the Quartering Act. Next, Parliament passed the Quebec Act, which removed the colony's charter and put them under the Quebec government's rule, which was known to be Catholic. The Protestants of Massachusetts were enraged at the prospect. The colony was cut off, and their fury was overwhelming. For the first time, the colonies had a common enemy—the mother country. The die was cast. The colonies were united in rage, and it was not long before they united in war.

A War Shaped by Landscape

War requires generals and other strategists to understand the geography and ecology of a landscape to best their enemy. Never was this so true as during the American

Henry Pelham was a Loyalist living in Boston in the years just prior to the Revolution. He was known by contemporaries for being kind and compassionate and loyal to the British crown, but he is rarely discussed by history textbooks or media. Ironically, it is likely that almost every American who has learned some early American history has seen his work. Pelham worked as an artist and cartographer—also known as a map maker—during the Revolution.

Pelham's map of Boston during the prerevolutionary era is considered one of the best maps of the region created from that time. As a resident of Boston, Pelham was well acquainted with the effect of the growing tension between the British and the Americans there. It was actually the closing of Boston Harbor in response to the Boston Tea Party that forced Pelham to turn to cartography to support himself because he could no longer run his business through the closed port.

Ultimately, Pelham became one of the most famous cartographers of the Revolution. His fame, however, could have been far greater. Pelham created one of the most iconic images of the American Revolution and never received credit for it. He produced the best-known engraving of the Boston Massacre, but the image was stolen.

Loyalist Henry Pelham's *The Fruits of Arbitrary Power* was stolen by Paul Revere and changed into *The Bloody Massacre in King-Street*, which was used to promote the Patriots' agenda.

Pelham's *The Fruits of Arbitrary Power* was commandeered by Patriot Paul Revere. Revere stole Pelham's work, altered it slightly, and created one of the most famous anti-British propaganda posters of the American Revolution from it: *The Bloody Massacre in King-Street*. Today, Revere's reproduction is considered one of the most famous and effective pieces of historical propaganda, and it was not even his own original work. Though Pelham fought Revere for the rights to his work, he was largely ignored.

Revolution. While every war requires a strategic knowledge of the land an army is fighting on, in the Revolution, such knowledge was pivotal to the ultimate results of the war. In fact, it is highly unlikely that without the American geography on their side, the Continental soldiers ever stood a chance. It was a war won through intrigue, deception, and a willingness to fight "unfairly"—something that the geography lent itself to and the Americans took advantage of repeatedly throughout the war.

Statistically speaking, from the very beginning, the odds of an American victory against the British was very unlikely. The British army was better trained, more experienced, and better funded, so how could the Continental Army stand a chance? The British had all of the tangible advantages. England was a superpower with an exceptional military and properly trained troops, while the Continental Army was a ragtag group of poorly trained, poorly equipped, and somewhat disorganized former farmers and citizens led by a former British officer. Furthermore, the British even held some of the most geographically and politically (geopolitically) influential lands during the war. For a majority of the war, New York City was a hotbed of Loyalist support in the heart of British territory. New York was a major port and gave strategic access and potential control of the Hudson River to the British. Had the British gained complete control of the river, they could have cut off access and supplies to most of New England, where the war was raging. By all measures, an American victory did not seem like a possibility, except that the American Revolution was fought unlike any war before.

More than anything, understanding the environment and geography of the land gave the Americans an important strategic advantage. The British army was used to traditional battle tactics. At the time, armies would meet in a large, open field; line up facing the opposing army; and fire their guns at each other. Therefore, the British were not prepared for American warfare. The East Coast of the United States was lined with thick forests that made formal battles impossible. Furthermore, Americans learned from Native Americans and adopted guerrilla warfare tactics, which consisted of sneak attacks and close-contact combat. This was completely alien to the dignified and traditional British military. Navigating the new terrain and the surprise guerrilla attacks of the American army ensured that the British soldiers were very far out of their comfort zone. In turn, familiarity with the terrain and a willingness to fight in what was considered less-than-gentlemanly warfare with surprise attacks ensured that the Americans were able to best the British.

The British disadvantage was further exacerbated by how far away their ruling body was. The distance that had motivated colonists to rebel also left the military adrift. Mail and information from the mother country took weeks—and sometimes months—to arrive because of the challenges of intercontinental travel. Delivering mail was a complex process that required a long sea voyage. Often, by the time orders were received, they were more than two months old, and the information was no longer relevant. On the other hand, the American military worked hard to deliver valuable, quick, and accurate information. Though both sides used spies to gather intelligence, the American spy ring, led by General George Washington, was very effective, and Washington demanded quick and accurate information above all else. That information never had to travel far.

American Climate

Early in American history, most land was uncleared forest, and not far from the seaboard the Appalachian Mountains provided their own barrier. For the Americans familiar with the territory, the terrain was navigable. Moving a huge, armed fleet with infantry like large and cumbersome cannons made travel through the region slow and arduous for the poorly prepared British military.

The environment of the United States in general was a burden on the British. The Americans were used to the weather and changing climates. The British were not.

George Washington ushered his troops across the Delaware River under the cover of darkness and fog during the Battle of Trenton.

The changing weather was difficult to adapt to, which only benefited the Americans. An example of this was the fog that regularly gathered over the Delaware River. Had fog not created sufficient cover for the American army's crossing of the Delaware in December of 1776, the war could have been over before it ever really began. The Americans would have been forced to face off against a very powerful battalion of Hessian soldiers (German mercenary soldiers) when the Continental soldiers were already bruised and battered and not at all prepared. Instead, using the fog that was common to that region for cover, the Americans snuck away in the middle of the night, surviving to fight another day.

In fact, the brutal cold of the northeastern winters also acted as an advantage. They gave the Continental Army the reprieve that Washington desperately needed to train his team of military misfits. Though the conditions were cold and miserable at Valley Forge in the winter of 1777–1778, with soldiers suffering from illness and wearing poor-quality uniforms and boots not well suited to the icy Pennsylvania weather, the cease-fire it created also granted Washington time for necessary training that helped set the tone for the second half of the war and assisted on the path to victory.

Ultimately, the strategic use of geography was one of the greatest strengths of the American army and Washington's leadership. Knowing the land and the climate helped the Americans win the war even with the odds stacked against them. Combined with French support that came later in the war, Americans' knowledge of the land paid off in a decisive victory. What could have been a disastrous defeat was instead the start of a nation. After the British defeat at Yorktown, peace came, and with it came a new country. The Treaty of Paris was signed in 1783, releasing Americans from British rule.

At the close of the American Revolution, the colonists were now citizens of a new nation. Quick to establish a governing body, the colonists signed the Articles of Confederation. Unfortunately, the Articles were very poorly equipped to sustain the new country. Though the colonies had unified in the name of revolution, in truth, each colony saw itself as a separate entity. The new states wanted controlling power in their own hands rather than held by the federal government. As a result, the states placed so little power in the hands of the federal government that they had rendered it much too weak. The federal government did not even have enough power to regulate international trade, and that was destroying the budding American economy. The Articles had to be replaced, and in 1789 the United States Constitution was ratified, this time with a federal government that was stronger and fit to govern a unified nation. The United States of America was born!

The United States of America

The new nation faced many challenging obstacles in its infancy. Each state was still very different from one another, and unity was hard to come by. The federal government was learning how to lead. Meanwhile, the Industrial Revolution was changing the Northern economy. Textile mills modeled after the British factories popped up along waterways. In the South, cotton was becoming big business thanks to the invention of the cotton gin, which made separating cotton seeds from the cotton much easier and faster. This fed the slave trade and reinforced the Southern plantation economy.

Furthermore, the tension with Native Americans increased as settlers moved into the frontier. The growing population pushed farther and farther west into the Ohio River Valley. With the influx of people moving west, regions that were formerly unsettled were now populated. The new country needed to figure out how to govern these regions. The issue was finally resolved when Congress passed the Ordinance of 1787, better known today as the Northwest Ordinance.

The Northwest Ordinance

According to the Northwest Ordinance, the federal government could sell land to settlers. When the land was first settled, the federal government appointed leaders in the different regions. Each region would have a governor with a secretary to the region and three judges for court proceedings. These people would select the laws for the region and enforce them, though Congress could overrule a law if needed. It was the governor's job to maintain a militia and resolve conflict with Native Americans. If, however, at least five thousand free men lived in the area, the local government would grow. At this time, they would elect a legislature that was similar to the federal government's House of Representatives. From there, if the territory ultimately grew to a population of sixty thousand people, it was then eligible to apply for statehood. This process required a constitutional convention to draft a state constitution, which then had to be approved by the federal government. The final edict was that slavery was illegal for all states in western regions.

Meriwether Lewis and William Clark explored the Louisiana Territory, and their efforts supported American expansionism.

Chapter Two

America's Footprint:
1800–1877

★ ★ ★ ★ ★ ★ ★

In the early 1800s, the population was growing and steadily spreading into the Mississippi River Valley and Appalachian Mountains. Then, a new opportunity to grow in a different direction arose in 1803. Under the guidance of the third president the United States, Thomas Jefferson, the nation acquired the Louisiana Territory from France for $15 million. Spanning more than 530,000,000 acres (214,483,390 ha), the Louisiana Purchase was a bargain. The US government paid about three cents (that would be sixty-four cents today) per acre for land that could easily accommodate about thirteen new states.

The purchase received some harsh criticism, however. Globally, the sale was contentious. The land was purchased

★ ★ ★ ★ ★ ★ ★

from Napoleon, who was growing increasingly powerful in Europe. This growing power was a source of concern worldwide. In the United States, some saw the purchase as an overstep of federal power. States were still hesitant to grant too much power to the federal government. As a strong supporter of state power over federal power himself, Jefferson was conflicted about the decision. He was unsure of whether the president could orchestrate land deals and purchases. Other member of Jefferson's political party, the Federalists, downright opposed it, but the purchase went through. It changed the map of America dramatically, nearly doubling the nation's landmass.

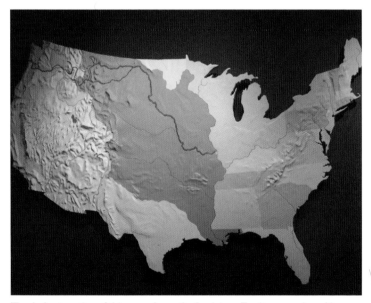

The darkest portion of this map shows the Louisiana Territory, purchased by Thomas Jefferson in 1803.

Uncharted Lands

★ ★

After the purchase of the Louisiana Territory, the United States now owned uncharted lands. Needing to understand what he had purchased, Jefferson employed frontiersman Meriwether Lewis to explore the new territory. In turn, Lewis enlisted the help of William Clark, a fellow frontiersman. The two led an entourage called the Corps of Discovery into the new region to discover what treasures and mysteries the territory held.

The Lewis and Clark expedition began in 1804 on the Ohio River, heading toward the Missouri River. They eventually worked their way in the direction of the Pacific Ocean, following river after river to try to catalogue the full extent of the newly purchased lands and its waterways.

Writing in journals and making sketches, the team documented each discovery as they traveled toward the Pacific Ocean. The expedition lasted more than two years and revealed some of the incredible features of what is today the American Midwest. Their journals describe the land, the climate, and the geography of the Louisiana Territory. They describe contact with Native Americans in the region as well as new species of plants and animals they found.

The Lewis and Clark expedition fed the American desire to grow. America was expanding, and Lewis and Clark's journey led the charge into the Midwest.

Cotton and Slavery

Slavery has left a lasting and painful mark on American history. As the United States grew, the debate over slavery became more and more passionate. In the 1800s, plantations covered the Southern states, where warmer climates allowed for long growing seasons and mass production of cash crops.

Enslaved Africans and African American people born into slavery were brutalized, abused, and dehumanized under the system. It was the unpaid labor force of slavery that enabled the Southern economy to make money, which made slavery very popular in the South. Though slavery was practiced in the country as a whole, the large plantation-style farming that was driven by slavery was characteristic of

This 1884 lithograph shows a cotton plantation on the Mississippi River during the antebellum period. Plantations were sites of terrible abuse and oppression.

the Southern states. After the American Revolution and into the nineteenth century, the inhumane treatment of enslaved people became a point of contention among different states. The country was divided over the legality of slavery and whether it should be permitted or not.

In 1807, the importation of enslaved people was outlawed in the United States of America. No new people could be brought into the country as slaves, though those who were currently enslaved—as well as their current and future children—were still considered property. With the end of the slave trade, each enslaved person became more valuable. A system arose in which owning slaves signified wealth, and wealth meant status. Banning the slave trade, rather than eradicating the system, commodified it further and added prestige to a heinous and abusive system where people were treated like chattel.

The excessive farming and overcultivation of the land in the south as a direct result of cotton and plantation-style farming also led to further problems. Overcultivation was killing the land and thereby putting further strain on the Southern economy. It stripped the once-fertile soil of its natural nutrients, which made growing crops increasingly challenging and the crop yields lower. As the country moved into the antebellum period (the period directly before the Civil War), Southern plantation owners began to look for new locations to move their plantations in hopes of revitalizing their economy. Land in more distant regions like Texas or even the Caribbean was favorable for its fertile soil, but the nation was forced to face how continued expansion of the country related to the issue of slavery. The Missouri Compromise was passed by Congress in 1819 in an attempt to solve the problem.

The Missouri Compromise

After the Louisiana Purchase doubled the United States's territory, debates over slavery became even more heated. The antislavery movement, led by abolitionists, grew ever louder and came to a head when Missouri petitioned to join the Union in 1819 as a slave state. Up until this point, there was an equal number of "free" states (states without slaves) and "slave" states. Maintaining that careful balance helped soothe an increasingly volatile situation. Adding Missouri tipped the balance.

To compensate for Missouri, Maine was also added to the Union but as a free state. To ensure the peace would remain as subsequent states were added to the Union, the territory acquired through the Louisiana Purchase was divided on the 36°30' parallel. Any state admitted above the line was a free state. Any state admitted below the line was a slave state. This model kept a tentative peace until it was overturned with the Kansas-Nebraska Act in 1854, but it was also a temporary solution for a bigger systemic problem. America was divided by more than the 36°30' parallel. Slavery and the tension around it was growing, splitting the nation into two camps: those against slavery and those for slavery.

A Growing Nation

The United States continued to expand at a rapid rate. In the same year that Missouri and Maine joined the Union, the country purchased another large plot of land. In the Adam-Onís Treaty of 1819 (also known as the Florida Purchase Treaty), the United States gained the remainder of Spanish holdings in the area that is today Florida. In exchange for the land, the United States took on Spanish debt to American citizens. These debts amounted to about $5 million but earned the nation another large region.

Meanwhile, the country as a whole was growing fast. The 1820s saw the country expanding well into the Midwest. Texas applied for statehood toward the end of the 1830s but was turned down. It was not until 1845 that Texas, formerly part of Mexico, was finally annexed into the United States. Under the expansionist president James K. Polk, America began to antagonize Mexico following Mexican raids in Texas. Finally, a battle broke out between the two countries along the border at the Rio Grande.

The Mexican-American War followed in 1846 and was all about expanding territory. In a series of battles in which the Unites States saw many victories, the war definitively favored the United States. In 1847, the United States attacked Mexico City, and that ended the war. With the signing of the Treaty of Guadalupe in 1848, the United States took a large swath of Mexico's territory, including what is today New Mexico, Arizona, Nevada, Utah, and California. Americans were dreaming of a country that spanned from coast to coast, and the new territory made it possible. In 1849, the discovery of gold in California fueled further dreams of expansion.

Manifest Destiny

Manifest Destiny was the belief that the United States was destined to span from the East Coast to the West Coast. Though there were many ideologies that were important and pivotal during the nineteenth century, none was so influential as Manifest Destiny. Many of the political moves of the century related to the goal of America spanning from the Atlantic to the Pacific.

When gold was discovered in California's Sacramento Valley, people flocked to the West Coast in what became known as the California gold rush. Within a year of finding the first nuggets of gold, the population grew one hundred

Boomtowns popped up in California as a direct result of the gold rush. Populations of barely settled areas skyrocketed and quickly became towns and cities, such as San Francisco, depicted here as it looked in 1849.

times over, spiking from one thousand nonnative people to about one hundred thousand by the end of the following year. Boomtowns popped up in California, fueled by Americans' desire to strike it rich.

Seeking the quickest route to gold and wealth, Americans started traveling by land in covered wagons in a mass migration to the western half of the United States. Known as the Oregon Trail, this transcontinental route began in Missouri and ran all the way to what is today Portland, Oregon. The route was 2,000 miles (3,200 kilometers) long and was filled with dangerous and difficult terrain. Travelers had to contend with Native Americans as they passed directly through Native territories when the trail crossed through prairies and the open landscape of the Midwestern states (specifically Kansas and Nebraska). Though this leg of the trip was flatter and easier to travel, it ended in mountainous terrain. Specifically, the trail headed into the rough lands of southern Wyoming toward the Rocky Mountains. The trail was made longer by the need to follow fresh water. The climate became increasingly dry as travelers made their way past Wyoming, and access to fresh water was essential for survival. Eventually, settlers were faced with crossing the Great Basin, known for its dry and arid climate, so following a path with water such as along the Snake River

This map by Ezra Meeker from 1907 shows the path of the Oregon Trail across the United States as a thick black line. Note that the trail has more than one origin point and breaks into different routes.

or Columbia River was the only option. While water tended to be scarce, food in this region was plentiful for those willing to hunt. After the Basin came the Blue Mountains in what is today Idaho. Eventually, a path was carved from there through the Cascades to the West Coast. The journey took months. If travelers timed it poorly, they could arrive in the mountains during winter conditions, which made the journey even more perilous.

The Oregon Trail was not one single trail but rather a path made up of many different trails. Regardless of which detour or path travelers followed, the trip was

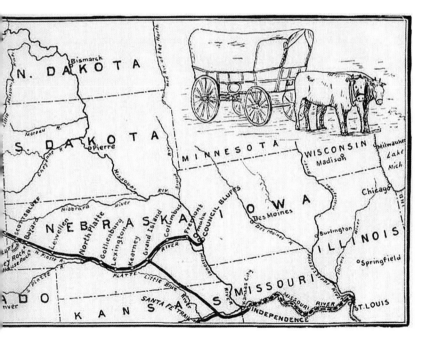

Westward expansion was felt most keenly by the Native American tribes that were increasingly displaced as a result of settlers moving west. Native Americans spent much of the nineteenth century resisting the United States's expansion. Skirmishes with settlers abounded, but American progress westward was relentless. One of the greatest atrocities committed by the United States against Native Americans during this time was President Andrew Jackson's Indian Removal Act of 1830.

The Indian Removal Act made it legal for the president to steal Native lands while forcing the Native tribes to relocate to other, often less desirable, lands. Though some tribes followed the orders and moved on their own, others did not. Most famous among the resistance were the Cherokee, who were later forcibly removed by the government in a march known as the "Trail of Tears." It is estimated that four thousand people died as a result of the march, which passed through what is today Alabama, Arkansas, Georgia, Illinois, Kentucky, Missouri, North Carolina, Oklahoma, and Tennessee and spanned nearly 2,200 miles (3,541 km). This relocation was just one example of different methods that the United States used to eradicate Native American culture. It was a true tragedy.

Though this portion of the Trail of Tears in Wynne, Arkansas, looks peaceful today, the forced relocation of Native Americans on that march remains a terrible atrocity in American history.

always long. It took anywhere from four to six months. The Oregon Trail, however, can be seen as a triumph of the era; it symbolized an ideology of the century. America had fulfilled its supposed destiny: the nation spanned from the Atlantic to the Pacific. Now the nation would face the challenge of how best to connect those coasts. That was where the railroad came in.

The railroad industry embodied the nineteenth century's ambition and met the need for an interconnected nation. Increased manufacturing in the North demanded easier and faster transport of goods to markets in the South and the Midwest. Cities were growing, and industrialization was leaving its mark on the nation as well. Railroads, in part, made that growth possible. Truthfully, very few technological innovations in United States had an impact equal to that of the railroad. The country was knitting together faster than ever and expanding by leaps and bounds, and the railroad was the missing link the nation needed to connect the country.

Steam Power

Railroads revolutionized travel in America, and the American railroad system really started to flourish in the late 1840s into the 1850s. Northern states in particular invested heavily in railroad infrastructure. Driven by

In the nineteenth century, railroads connected the country unlike ever before.

manufacturing needs, railroads provided fast and effective shipping options to markets. Trips that once took days now took mere hours. For a nation growing at the rapid rate that the United States was, railroads became essential.

Steam technology like trains and steamboats connected the country more effectively than any other transportation had before. Canals were built, and steamships dominated the waterways. Then, railroads conquered the land by connecting the North with the Midwest and some of the South.

Finally, in 1862, the Central Pacific and Union Pacific Railroad Companies broke ground on the transcontinental railroad. When it was finished, it connected the country from coast to coast in an unprecedented feat of ingenuity. Ironically, as the railroads ensured the nation became more and more geographically connected, social and political tension over the issue of slavery left the North and the South more divided than ever before.

The Path to Civil War

Tensions about slavery boiled over in 1854 when Congress passed the Kansas-Nebraska Act. The Kansas-Nebraska Act declared that Kansas and Nebraska could join the Union and decide for themselves whether they would be slave states or free states. The vote in Kansas was a catastrophe that ultimately resulted in Kansas having two opposing legislatures, one on each side of the slavery argument. Eventually, Kansas resolved the issue and was added to the Union as a free state, but the Kansas-Nebraska Act had overturned the Missouri Compromise. The tentative peace and calm that had come with the Missouri agreement was no longer in place.

To make the tension worse, Northern states had fully embraced modernization and industrialization. Their diversified economy was booming. On the other hand, the Southern economy was still centered on plantation-based farming. Steadfastly committed to a slavery-based economy, the South had not industrialized and was still entirely dependent on slave labor. As resistance against slavery grew, the Southerners risked losing their economy. Threats to secede from the Union became more and more vocal and common, until they came to fruition with the election of Republican Abraham Lincoln as president in 1860. The Republican Party was avidly antislavery, and the Southern states chose to leave the Union rather than risk losing what they saw as their way of life. South Carolina was the first to secede in December of 1860, followed by Mississippi, Florida, Alabama, Georgia, and Louisiana, which all seceded in January of 1861. Texas followed suit in February of 1861. Half of Virginia seceded in April of that year, followed by Arkansas and North Carolina in May. Tennessee joined the Confederacy in June of that year. Together, these states created their own nation, the Confederate States of America.

The Union and the Confederacy

The Civil War was the bloodiest war in American history, with 620,000 dead by its end in 1864. The enemy was not a foreign entity; instead, brothers and other family members fought against each other. People were killing their fellow countrymen. President Lincoln worked hard to bring the war to a swift conclusion. He used the newly invented telegraph to keep up to date in real time, something never imagined in previous eras. The telegraph made coordinating and strategizing easier than ever and enabled the North to carefully orchestrate its movements and attacks. Thanks to the telegraph, newspapers were able to report on the destruction and loss that came from a nation divided by war.

The war destroyed infrastructure, farm land, and communities. A majority of the battles were fought in Southern states near the Union's southern border. Maryland and Tennessee saw a great number of battles. Northern Virginia, which had not seceded when the western portion of the state had, was ravaged by the Confederacy. In return, the Union used a scorched-earth model of warfare and burned farms and plantations through states like Georgia and North Carolina. This was a direct attack on the Southern economy and was what eventually forced the South to surrender.

Union generals attacked the weak points of the South and made their opponents vulnerable by blocking Confederate ports. Then, they destroyed the South's main source of income—the plantations. Unlike the North, the South did not have much infrastructure that enabled trade without ports, and there was no other industry to sustain the economy when the farms were burned. The railroad industry had not taken off in the South, and the entire economy was dependent on slavery. Meanwhile, the Union used railroads to run supplies down to the battles. Manufacturing was focused on the war effort in the North, and businesses stayed open there. The South, however, was good at two things, farming and slavery, and both of them went up in smoke in the Civil War.

The end of the Civil War saw a chance at a new beginning, and it was undeniable that the country was changed by the experience. Now, there was an opportunity to be reborn as a new nation. The United States just had to choose a model for becoming whole once again.

New York City, seen here as it was in 1880, was a prime example of the wealth of the Gilded Age. Mansions sprang up, and titans of industry transformed the American economy and landscape.

★ Chapter Three ★

A Time for Rebuilding: 1877–1945

★ ★ ★ ★ ★ ★ ★

In 1865, when the Civil War was finally and truly over, the United States of America was a completely different place from when the war started. Around 620,000 people had died, and the country's president, Abraham Lincoln, was dead by assassination. The South was ravaged. The former economic model dependent on slavery was outlawed, and the land was destroyed by war. In the short years following the final Confederate surrender by General Robert E. Lee, change swept the nation. The Confederacy was forced to rejoin the Union, and the laws of the United States had been updated. The Constitution was amended three times in the first five years after the war. The Thirteenth Amendment abolished slavery, the Fourteenth declared

★ ★ ★ ★ ★ ★ ★

African Americans as citizens with rights protected by the federal government, and finally, the Fifteenth Amendment granted all men the right to vote regardless of race or color. In a way, by 1870, the country was starting over, created something new from the wreckage of the catastrophic war. It was time to start rebuilding.

Reconstruction

The Reconstruction period lasted through March of 1877. It was a time to try to reunify the nation after the Civil War. Reconstruction was largely a plan to reintegrate Southern states into the Union. During this period, Southern states were forced to ratify the Thirteenth Amendment and pushed back by passing local legislation called "black codes," which oppressed and stripped African Americans of the rights that were newly granted to them by the Reconstruction Amendments. Many black codes targeted rights like voting. Such laws were forerunners and early versions of Jim Crow laws, which would begin the legal and systematic racial segregation of black and white people that characterized the American South during much of the twentieth century.

The racist black codes were a form of Southern resistance against what was known as Radical Reconstruction, or Congressional Reconstruction. Congress divided the South into five military zones controlled by Union generals.

According to the plan, cooperation would eventually help them gain state status. Another part of the Reconstruction plan was the creation of the Freedmen's Bureau, which was designed to support the newly free men as they navigated society as well as supply them acreage to farm. This acreage was never granted, but the program did provide education to many African Americans who had previously been forbidden from receiving schooling. It was a step toward the necessary equality that the Southern states were so resistant to and actively tried to prevent.

Urbanization

While the South was renegotiating its place in the Union, other big changes were afoot in the country. The era following the Civil War was characterized by industrialization and mechanized production, which were growing increasingly popular, as were cities. Before the Civil War, 87 percent of the population lived in towns and regions with fewer than eight thousand people. In the years following the Civil War, urban populations more than doubled. By 1900, the popularity of cities had skyrocketed with about 40 percent of the population living in cities as a part of urbanization. The population as a whole nearly tripled from thirty-one million in 1860 to more than ninety million by 1910.

Jim Crow laws in the south acted as a form of legal racial segregation to oppress African Americans even after the Reconstruction Amendments declared them free citizens. In 1892, Homer Plessy, a man of mixed race, boarded a train in Louisiana, a state that had a Separate Car Act. Plessy sat in the "white only" car and refused to move to the "black only" car when approached. Plessy was arrested, and the case made it all the way to the Supreme Court with Homer Plessy asserting that the segregation of the Separate Car Act violated the Thirteenth and Fourteenth Amendments. In 1896, the Supreme Court ruled, "That it does not conflict with the Thirteenth Amendment, which abolished slavery and involuntary servitude." They also elaborated on the Fourteenth Amendment, saying, "By the Fourteenth Amendment, all persons born or naturalized in the United States, and subject to the jurisdiction thereof, are made citizens of the United States … and the states are forbidden from making or enforcing any law which shall abridge the privileges or immunities of citizens in the United States." The court ruled that the separation of cars did not violate the Fourteenth Amendment because:

The object of the amendment was undoubtedly to enforce the absolute equality of the two races before the law, but in the nature of things, it could not have been intended to abolish distinctions based upon color, or to enforce social, as distinguished from political, equality, or commingling of the two races upon terms unsatisfactory to either. Laws permitting, and even requiring, their separation, in places where they are liable to be brought into contact, do not necessarily imply the inferiority of either race to the other, and have been generally, if not universally, recognized as within the competency of the state legislatures in the exercise of their powers.

This essentially culminated in a ruling saying that so long as the amenities were of equal quality, segregation was legal within the bounds of the Constitution. The *Plessy v. Ferguson* ruling became the standard for legalizing racial segregation in almost all forms of public infrastructure across the South for the next half century. Racial segregation applied to almost every aspect of public life in cities and towns across the South until the 1950s. In 1954, the ruling of "separate but equal" was overturned in the case of *Brown v. the Board of Education*. In that case, the Supreme Court acknowledged that very act of separating people based on race and skin color was inherently unequal and a violation of the rights of the segregated people.

New York City in 1900

A large motivator behind this population shift was the industrialization of the period. Farming became easier with new technology, which meant fewer people had to farm to create the same or even larger yields than in years prior. There was less money in farming, and a surplus of farmers moved into cities, seeking work in new industrial markets. In many cases, industrial work consisted of monotonous jobs that required less backbreaking work than farming because machines replaced manual labor. It became the "American Dream" to achieve wealth like the tycoons who led the Industrial Revolution with railroad investing, oil production, and new industrial markets. The increased population also led to growth in new industries. Luxuries like electric lighting and indoor plumbing became

American Geography and the Environment

commonplace. Skyscrapers made of steel were built ever-higher while bridges stretched across rivers, connecting routes quickly and efficiently. Cities like New York became hotbeds for money making.

Industrialization was fully embraced and changed the United States population irrevocably. There were huge shifts in demographics. This so-called Gilded Age marked a new model for the American landscape and created new social classes. The middle class rose and grew with increased industry, while a new demographic—the working poor—grew rapidly. To accommodate the growing populations, squalid tenement apartments became typical among the poor and lower classes. It was a new social, cultural, and political environment different from what had existed before in America.

Progressivism and Conservation

With a changing society came changing ideology. The struggles of the lower classes and factory laborers as well as the increased corruption in big business became the primary focus of Progressives into the twentieth century. Increased demands for workers' and human rights and reform to society led to improvements in cities. Progressivism and widespread reform of the early twentieth century also turned its critical lens to the environment and sparked an increased interest in environmental issues and conservation.

A byproduct of industrialization and mechanization was increased waste. Large-scale factories and railroads created smog and polluted the air. Increased logging for construction led to deforestation. The environment of the United States was being dramatically impacted by humans and their work. An example could be seen in the herds of American bison across the Great Plains—once plentiful and healthy, their numbers dwindled thanks to the American railroad system, which had infringed on their habitat and led to increased hunting.

Famous legislation passed under progressive government officials like President Theodore Roosevelt aimed to protect the country's natural resources and splendor well into the future. Such legislation included,

Yellowstone National Park

but was not limited to, the New Lands Act in 1902, which created funds for irrigation projects from federal land sales, and the creation of the Inland Waterways Commission in 1907, which was responsible for studying natural power sources, water transportation, and forests, rivers, and soil. The National Conservation Commission, established in 1909, was primarily focused on long-term planning for the preservation of national lands and resources. It was also during this era that many national and state parks were founded, protecting national lands and the species that lived there. The National Parks Service and the US Forest Services were created to protect the parks. These paired well with the National Monuments Act, also known as the Antiquities Act, which granted the president the power to restrict the use of national lands that had prehistoric and historical relevance or were valuable for scientific study. It was through this act that President Roosevelt preserved and protected 150 million acres (60,702,846 ha) of forest and created many national parks and national monuments for future generations to enjoy.

World War I

The United States was drawn into World War I by German attacks on American submarines in 1917. The war had raged in Europe since 1914, but under the leadership of President Woodrow Wilson, America stayed out of the conflict until direct German antagonization and violence occurred. Unlike in Europe, the Americans were not directly on the frontlines. Instead, the environmental impact was felt in the United States more through the rationing of food, goods, and resources in support of the war effort and through increasing numbers of women in the workforce. Propaganda promoted the rationing of goods and resources like wheat, meat, fat, and sugar, which were

Technology changed the way war was fought during World War I. Here, soldiers of different nations wear the gas masks that helped them survive.

supplied for the war effort to stem the increasing demands for food for troops and Europeans whose farmlands were being decimated by battle. Rationing continued even after the war to help feed starving Europeans in the wake of the war's destruction.

A greater effect was felt in the United States after the end of the war. World War I was the first modern war fought with highly effective weaponry, like machine guns and caustic gases. These innovations led to devastatingly high international death counts. Approximately 9.1 million people died in the war, and those who survived lived with the trauma of watching friends suffer. Those who managed to make it home from the war most desired finding peace. Presidential candidate Warren G. Harding won his campaign with his push for a "return to normalcy."

American citizens wanted to begin enjoying life and experiencing the freedom of peace after the pressure and trauma of international war. American society embraced the "normalcy" and threw themselves full force into living again.

The Roaring Twenties

The 1920s was marked by a culture of fast living. It was also an era of high productivity and increased consumerism as many new products arrived on the market. Credit was extended widely—it seemed like everyone had credit and used it to buy, buy, buy. American manufacturing grew to keep pace with demand. For a time, it seemed like the economy would keep climbing to new heights. However, the growth and prosperity of the 1920s was unsustainable and would not last.

In addition to the widespread use of credit, stocks—which had to be backed by currency to maintain their value—were being bought on margin. This meant that people put a down payment on a stock and paid it off like a line of credit. In turn, this system led to rapid inflation. Inflation would have been sustainable if stocks' value had been backed by currency instead of credit. In reality, stocks were dangerously unstable. The economy continued to climb rapidly, which made for even more buying and spending, worsening the problem. It was a disaster waiting to happen, but the American public that had been disillusioned by war was seeking the comfort of the apparent success and affluence presented by the "Roaring Twenties." Politicians fed into ideas of American prosperity, including the 1928 presidential candidate Herbert Hoover. Hoover won the election based on his idealistic propaganda promising "a chicken in every pot and a car in every garage." What the economy served up instead was a massive disaster.

The Roaring Twenties came to a roaring halt in October of 1929, when the excessive use of credit caught up with the country. Known as Black Thursday, on October 24, 1929, the New York Stock Exchange saw a sudden and massive drop in stock value: a 25 percent decrease and $30 billion ($432 billion in modern currency) loss in a mere four days. People lost everything, and banks did not have the cash reserves to back the money people had stored in them.

The Great Depression

The stock market crash sent the United States into a downward spiral and ultimately sent a struggling economy into a deep depression. An earlier correction in the market (a drop in the value of overvalued stocks that spans several weeks) during March of 1929 had left the economy vulnerable and unemployment rates rising. The stock market crash that occurred in October would decimate the American economy for the next ten years. The Great Depression was in full swing and would dramatically change America and the world.

In direct contrast to the vivaciousness of the 1920s, the 1930s were marked by extreme economic instability. Banks went out of business. Unemployment skyrocketed to an incredible 25 percent, and the economy stagnated because no one had money to spend. People were not optimistic about the future, and many adopted a migratory lifestyle, seeking work in an economy that could not possibly support more jobs. The adage of "you must spend money to make money" is true when it comes to job creation. Money must be made off of consumer spending to pay employees, but if no one has money to spend, no new jobs enter the economy. Without people spending money, the economy could not pull itself out of the Depression and get people back to work. It was a dark time that seemed to have no end in sight.

The Dust Bowl

Drought in the Southern Plains made the Depression worse. Farmers had overcultivated the land during the massive drive to produce more and more wheat to feed the demands of a growing population. They hadn't let the land lie fallow and rejuvenate itself. The farmers overplowed the region too. The plains needed thick grasses to prevent erosion in times of drought. Otherwise, the winds that blew forcefully across the land would do a great deal of damage. Instead, the overplowed land was defenseless against the hot sun and forceful wind. Without rain, the plains dried up. Rich topsoil dried out and became dust. When high winds rose up, they dragged up large swells

A dust cloud threatens southeastern Colorado in 1936.

Hoovervilles

Some of the most iconic images of the Great Depression capture the realities of the shantytowns that popped up across the nation. Widespread unemployment meant that people did not have money to pay rent or mortgages, leading to a homeless population reaching unprecedented proportions. Millions of people lost their homes and were forced to find other places to live. The homeless and unemployed people who could not find another place to live formed communities of varying sizes and constructed haphazard shelters to protect themselves from the elements. These shantytowns could consist of just a few temporary structures or be massive communities with thousands of people living there. The structures were made of whatever supplies residents could find or afford at the time of construction. There was no plumbing, and dirt floors were common.

President Herbert Hoover, who had promised a "chicken for every pot," became a mockery. The country plummeted further and further into the Depression while people waited desperately for the government to come and save them. Instead, the government, personified by Hoover, failed them. The efforts he did make—like some public

People used whatever could be scavenged to build shanties during the Great Depression. Shantytowns became known as "Hoovervilles," after President Hoover.

works projects and decreasing taxes—did not alleviate the suffering. Hoover was extremely financially conservative in a time when Americans were desperately seeking assistance and aid in the form of goods like food and shelter. The American people felt abandoned when they most needed strong and supportive government. Inhabitants of these shantytowns dubbed them "Hoovervilles" as a jab at the person they saw as responsible for leaving them to their suffering. They wanted the name to reflect their extreme dissatisfaction with Hoover and his leadership.

of that dust from the dehydrated ground and whipped it through the air in massive dark clouds. These dust storms consisted of thick walls of dirty air that blew through the region and coated everything, including the lungs of humans and livestock alike. These winds killed many and destroyed what crops managed to grow in the dry dirt. What once had been a fertile land of wheat and grain, which had given the region the nickname "the bread basket," was now a dry and barren wasteland.

Faced with food shortages, unemployment, and deadly dust storms, some people migrated out. The drought lasted for years, leaving those who remained more and more destitute.

FDR and the New Deal

President Herbert Hoover left office as a disgrace in the eyes of the people but was replaced by a First Family who managed to provide something desperately needed in such dark times: hope. President Franklin Delano Roosevelt (FDR) and First Lady Eleanor Roosevelt, who was savvy and equally diligent in her efforts to save the nation, managed to give the United States something to believe when Roosevelt took office in 1932.

FDR quickly implemented the New Deal. Designed to provide immediate relief as well as help the economy recover over time, the New Deal changed the American

Many public works projects, like the one that created the Chickamauga Dam in Tennessee, were funded by Roosevelt's New Deal.

government and financial system. The New Deal created forty-seven new federal programs designed to help the economy stabilize. These programs outlined public works projects and provided funds to stimulate manufacturing in waves. Recovery was treated as a long-term project, one that required spending large amounts of money in hopes of jumpstarting the economy again. From closing banks, to government pay cuts to finance New Deal programs, FDR came to office ready to change the system, amass money, and start spending. Through legislation, FDR did everything he could to help—from creating jobs to bailing out and subsidizing farmers. He knew the country had to get back to work if they wanted to pull out of the Depression.

Under the New Deal, Roosevelt created the Civilian Conservation Corps (CCC). The CCC specifically targeted the environmental catastrophe of the Dust Bowl. The government also funded the creation of New Deal infrastructure like building new roads and bridges, hanging power lines, and building dams. The New Deal was a huge and unprecedented effort that also improved the quality of life for civilians in many different states and regions. It did manage to get many people back to work, but the New Deal alone was not enough to solve a problem the size of the Great Depression. There was no way that public works projects could have spent the kind of money necessary to really restore the country's economy and the world economy. It was World War II that ultimately ended the dire economic situation.

World War II

World War II was expensive. The massive amount of money spent in rapid succession—both nationally and globally—finally pulled the world out of the economic downward spiral it had been in since 1929. The start of World War II in 1939 signaled the beginning of a huge shift in global politics, but it was not until Japan, a member of the Axis Powers, bombed Pearl Harbor on December 7, 1941, that the United States entered the war.

Though Americans were late to join, they were instrumental in ending the conflict. On August 6, 1945, President Harry S. Truman ordered the dropping of an atomic bomb on the Japanese city of Hiroshima. An estimated eighty thousand people were killed instantly, many from the explosive heat of the radiation. About 67 percent of the city was destroyed. A second, smaller bomb was dropped on the city of Nagasaki on August 9, 1945. Around forty thousand people died, and the bomb wiped out nearly one-third of the city in seconds, with much more of the city left damaged. No weapon had ever wreaked such havoc and destroyed so much so quickly. Though the bombs finally ended a war that seemed ceaseless, they did so at such a horrid cost that the damage can never be undone. Nuclear weapons were now a key part of geopolitics. They brought the power to not only end a war but potential to be the end of the world as a whole. The threat of nuclear war and its potential effects would haunt and dictate the United States' foreign policy from then on.

The United States dropped an atomic bomb on the Japanese city of Nagasaki on August 9, 1945. Pictured here is Nagasaki Medical College in the aftermath. All of the wooden buildings on the campus were instantly destroyed, leaving only a few decimated buildings remaining.

Chapter Four

America Today: 1945–Present

★ ★ ★ ★ ★ ★ ★

F ear of nuclear war motivated a great deal of the United States' foreign policy after World War II. This fear, along with the fear of communism, impacted the country's international politics for much of the twentieth century. Communism and nuclear war were seen as a threat to America's status as a superpower. A new monster, nuclear weaponry, had been unleashed on the world, and it had the power to decimate the American way of life, liberty, and land like nothing else ever before.

The Cold War

In the twentieth century, the United States cast itself into the role of global defender of democracy. The Soviet Union

★ ★ ★ ★ ★ ★ ★

was spreading communism in Europe, and the Soviet Union had developed nuclear weaponry as well. These two superpowers, the United States and the Soviet Union, spent the second half of the twentieth century facing off.

Containment

One of the biggest problems of the Cold War was that the United States of America could not afford to go to war with the Soviet Union, and the Soviet Union could not afford to go to war with America. The risk was too high for each country and the world as a whole. Both superpowers had nuclear weapons, and the destruction that such warfare would cause, not just to each nation but to the world, ensured that neither nation wanted war to actually break

Joseph Stalin led the Soviet Union until his death in 1953.

out. That said, there was a continued and dangerous tension between the two superpowers consistently from the 1950s all the way through the 1980s. The threat of nuclear war rose and fell, and each country postured politically against the other, but neither ever declared war on the other.

Americans did not trust communism, so they watched the Soviet Union closely. This close scrutiny reached a fever pitch as Soviet influence rose in Europe. After World War II, the Soviets began spreading communism to smaller nations in Europe and supporting communist uprisings in those nations. For a nation as loyal to the concepts of democracy and free markets as the United States, the spread of communism was seen as a threat to everything the country had believed in since its founding. Furthermore, Soviet leader Joseph Stalin committed atrocities against the Soviet people.

To the Soviet Union, the United States represented a democracy with free markets that were unregulated by government, which threatened the Soviet ideologies of socialism and communism. Basically, the Cold War was a passionate clashing of ideologies.

While the United States and the Soviet Union could not engage directly in battle, they spent the second half of the twentieth century influencing other nations. The United States' policy of indirect influence was known as the Cold War policy of containment. Cold War containment was essentially the United States trying to stop the spread of Soviet communism in Europe and the Middle East without ever formally engaging and declaring war against the Soviet Union. The United States found it could disrupt the spread of communism without outright engaging with the Soviet Union. This strategy saw the United States involved in three distinct wars completely outside its geographic borders.

The first conflict was the Korean War, which lasted from 1950 to 1953. After World War II, Korea was divided. The United States supported anticommunist interests in South Korea, and the Soviets backed the communist regime in North Korea. When combat stopped, Korea was officially split in two. The North was communist; the South was democratic. The two Koreas remain separate to this day, with North Korea closed to outside influence. (In a landmark international event, the two Koreas made peaceful contact for the first time since 1953 when South Korea hosted the Olympics in 2018.)

The second indirect face-off between the Soviets and the Americans took place in Vietnam, starting in 1954. The Vietnam War lasted for more than a decade, until US troops pulled out of the country in 1973. This conflict, above all others, is one of the most contested and protested conflicts in American history. Few people understood America's backing of the South Vietnamese

The United States used napalm in Vietnam. Napalm kills by burning and asphyxiating its victims.

who, though democratic, did not have the national majority's support within Vietnam. The communist Viet Minh were significantly more popular within the country. Furthermore, the war was exceptionally violent with a great deal of close-contact fighting because of the country's jungle terrain. Media footage of the war showed the horrors of napalm and landmines, and it was all happening just to stop communism. This, combined with the draft, made the war incredibly controversial in the United States. Many Americans protested US involvement in Vietnam throughout the 1960s. Had it not been for Soviet support of the Viet Minh, it is not likely that the United States would ever have been involved.

The Cuban Missile Crisis

The closest the United States of America came to nuclear war with the Soviet Union was the Cuban Missile Crisis in 1962. In now-declassified notes from the incident, Soviet influence in Cuba is obvious, and America intelligence tried to track the situation as closely as possible. One note from the file stated:

Soviet shipping and [blacked out] messages of 23 September indicate that the cargo ship Atkarsk had arrived that day in Port Nikolaev (the primary Soviet Black Sea port for loading arms for export) to load 2,454 tons of "Yastrobov's" cargo and was scheduled to arrive in Cuba between 21 and 31 October. (Yastrobov, a Soviet trade official, has been associated with the export of Soviet military cargo from Port Nikolaev since 1956.) These messages also reveal that the cargo ship Nikolaj [illegible], (which loaded 3,234 tons of unknown cargo in Nikolaev 9 to 16 September), would arrive in Cuba between 10 and 20 October.

Communications intelligence also indicates that the Soviet ship Kirov is probably now en route to Cuba, possibly carrying arms, and that another ship (Leninogorsk) is now loading cargo at Niklaev for Cuba.

(Two Soviet ships are known to have delivered military equipment to Cuba; the [Illegible] on 8 September and the Solnechnogorsk on 23 September.)

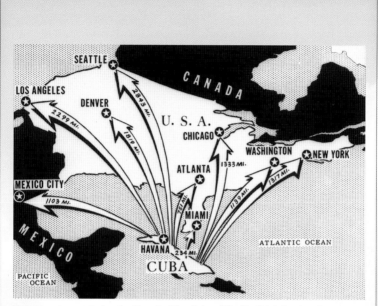

This map demonstrates the threat of the Cuban Missile Crisis by showing many potential missile paths.

What this formerly top-secret brief expresses is not only how imminent nuclear war was, but also how closely America was watching global and Soviet affairs. They had to; the threat was too great not to. In the case of the Cuban Missile Crisis, the missiles were on a Cuban beach 90 miles (145 km) from the United States' shores. Such close contact had potential to cause incredible and irreversible damage. President John F. Kennedy handled the crisis well with a calm show of confidence as well as an agreement to remove United States' missiles from Turkey. Both Cuba and Turkey were disarmed, and the United States and Soviets fell back into a cautious stalemate.

The final indirect clash between the Soviet Union and the United States took place in the 1980s. At the end of 1979, the Soviet Union invaded Afghanistan to try to support the communist Afghan government, which was failing to win battles against mujahideen rebels. In turn, the United States backed the mujahideen, partially because the United States wanted to protect its oil interests in the Middle East. Unfortunately for the communist Afghani government, the Soviet Union was in decline and continued to weaken during the 1980s. Though Soviets remained as a presence in the country until 1989, doing so fueled the demise of the Soviet Union. Splitting interests between Afghanistan and the mother country had stretched the declining nation too thin. Afghanistan fell into civil war among Afghan warlords while the Soviets were forced to pull out of the country. The Soviets, however, were too late in pulling out to even save their own government. The Soviet Union dissolved a few short years later in 1992, which finally ended the Cold War once and for all.

What is so important about all of these conflicts is that they showed a change in United States foreign policy. While previously the United States had tried to avoid international intervention and followed a policy of strict isolationism, these interactions were markers of change in international diplomacy. Now, the United States was directly involving itself in the foreign policy of other nations.

American Geography and the Environment

It was a complete about-face from the earlier geographic and political behavior that had defined American politics. However, the second half of the twentieth century was an era of change for more than just politics.

The Counterculture and Environmental Activism

During the 1960s, a new sociopolitical culture arose in the United States, one defined by protest. The counterculture, as it came to be known, was composed of people who protested the social and political abuses of the 1960s. It was an era of social consciousness and change. The counterculture was driven by a push for civil rights for African Americans, a

Activists protest the Boston Edison Company in 1969.

resistance to the Vietnam War, and an increasingly loud cry for conservation and environmental activism. By this point in American history, the country was fully industrialized, and manufacturing was the bedrock of the American economy. However, manufacturing's effect was already being felt.

Activists, seeing the effects of the industrialization on the environment, began to speak out against pollution and demanded clean air and clean water legislation. Writer Rachel Carson published her book *Silent Spring*, which explained the dangerous effects that pesticides like DDT had on the environment. The public was also increasingly concerned about the disposal of toxic waste that was created as a byproduct of nuclear power and the effects of that nuclear waste on the earth and human health. These activists even began decrying the dangers of greenhouse gases and the effects of ozone depletion—concerns that continue on today.

The United States government was quick to act on environmentalists' demands. Important environmental regulation and preservation included the passage of the Water Quality Act in 1965, which standardized water purity requirements in every state. Two years later, the Air Quality Act and Clean Air Act were also passed to protect against air pollution.

Congress also continued with conservation efforts such as those completed by President Theodore Roosevelt in the 1920s. Congress created the National Wilderness

Preservation System in 1964 and established more state and national parks. They also signed legislation to further protect parks that were already in existence.

Many of the issues that drew concern in the 1960s and 1970s are still prevalent today. Concerns like global warming and governmental protection of state and federal lands have been joined with an ongoing hunt for renewable and sustainable energies. Research in solar and wind power has seen some success, and increased use of more sustainable fuels like biofuels made from corn and sorghum are becoming popular. The hope is that renewable, sustainable resources will decrease dependence on nonrenewable energy sources like oil, which is limited in quantity and produces greenhouses gases when burned.

Land and Oil

The mentality of Manifest Destiny did not completely die out once the United States reached shore to shore, and its continued impact shaped today's America. States like Alaska and Hawaii were late to be added to the Union but were a direct result of the Manifest Destiny period.

In 1867, the country purchased of a large stretch of very northern land (586,412 square miles; 1,518,800 square km) from Russia, under the guidance of Abraham Lincoln's secretary of state, William Henry Seward. With a price tag

In the modern era, the United States has become a postindustrial society that is increasingly focused on and divided over environmental issues, specifically global warming. Scientific evidence points to the fact that burning fossil fuels for energy creates increased levels of carbon dioxide and greenhouse gases, which then deplete the atmospheric ozone layer. The ozone protects Earth from dangerous UVA and UVB light rays produced by the sun. As the ozone depletes, Earth's temperature rises from increased exposure to UVA and UVB rays that become trapped within the atmosphere because of the increasingly large layer of greenhouse gases.

These rising temperatures are melting polar icecaps, which raises sea levels and changes ecosystems essential to life on Earth. Global warming poses a huge threat to human life if not regulated, but some politicians argue that global warming is a natural process. While atmospheric warming is a natural process, the rate at which Earth's atmosphere

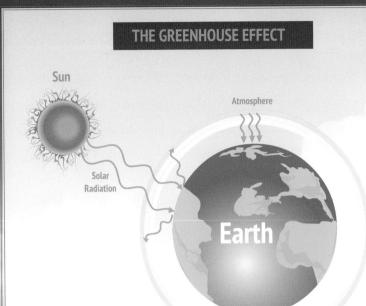

THE GREENHOUSE EFFECT

Sun

Atmosphere

Solar
Radiation

Earth

UVA and UVB rays produced by the sun are being trapped in Earth's atmosphere by a layer of greenhouse gases created by human pollution. This is raising the temperature of Earth's atmosphere, surface, and waters.

is heating is not natural and is a result of human processes. Failure to correct and protect against further warming could be catastrophic for fragile ecosystems that make life on Earth possible.

of $7.2 million (nearly $117 million in today's dollars) for the whole stretch, Seward paid about two cents an acre. The American public, however, did not see the value in the land and called the purchase "Seward's Folly" because of the icy terrain and cold Nordic landscape. Alaska would not become a state for several decades, until 1959. The true value of the land was not determined until 1986 when oil was found in Alaska, turning the former folly into one of the most lucrative purchases in history. The untapped oil reserves and resources in Alaska are massive, amounting to billions of barrels of oil. Today, oil is the state's greatest source of revenue.

As oil is power, literally and metaphorically, it is no surprise that the stores in Alaska would be so highly valued. For that matter, the United States has gone to war more than once to protect oil access overseas. At the end of the Cold War, when the United States and the Soviet Union clashed over Soviet presence in Afghanistan, one of the largest motivators for American involvement was not just preventing the spread of communism, it was the desire to protect oil interests in the Middle East. Such interest in the Middle East is a theme in American international politics in the decades surrounding the turn of the millennium.

After the Taliban-sponsored terror attack on the United States on September 11, 2001, the nation invaded Afghanistan in search of Osama bin Laden just a few days later. The war that followed, the Iraq War, has less direct ties to terrorism than the invasion of Afghanistan and can be partially explained by oil interests. Though Saddam Hussein was a dictator, American involvement was likely linked to the desire to protect these interests. With a majority of American oil coming out of Iraq at the time, it was important to make sure that the Iraqi government was friendly toward Americans.

The post–September 11 period also led to increased American interest in alternative power sources. Dependency on oil ensured American dependency on the Middle East, which can be dangerous in light of the changing political powers and rise of terrorist groups in the region. Since the beginning of the twenty-first century, oil has fluctuated in price, usually spiking around times of war and after terror attacks. The unstable price of oil gives a lot of control over the American economy to oil markets off American shores. Oil can be also be dangerous to the very land it comes from.

An example of the threat oil poses to the natural world can be seen in the effects of the 2010 BP oil spill in the Gulf of Mexico. A large oil leak sprang from an underwater pipe after an oil rig owned by BP exploded. The leak spread 3.19 million barrels of oil into the Gulf, causing a disaster of epic proportions. The oil spill killed animals, destroyed coral reefs, and decimated the ecosystems of the region.

Oil also washed ashore, spreading further problems. Even the chemical dispersants used to break up the oil were damaging, and the effects of the spill were still present in 2018.

Modern States and Territories

Alaska was not the end of America's efforts to expand. Hawaii, for instance, was added as a US territory in 1898. The queen of Hawaii, Liliuokalani, was overthrown by pineapple planters in 1893, which would eventually lead to Hawaii applying for annexation. Hawaii became a state at the same time Alaska did (1959), but it was not the United States' only tropical holding then or now.

Over time, America claimed several islands that are known today as unincorporated territories. These regions are governed by the United States Constitution but are not considered states, and the people of these regions, though for the most part considered citizens, do not have legal voting rights in United States elections unless they move to a legal state. (There is also one incorporated territory: Palmyra Atoll, which is a part of the Hawaiian Island chain but is not considered a part of the state of Hawaii.) These regions are largely independent, but they are also still considered as part of the country and so are protected by the United States.

Puerto Rico is an unincorporated American territory that was added to the American holdings around the time Hawaii was. Puerto Rico is a commonwealth, and residents of Puerto Rico are US citizens. Occasionally, this particular territory hosts a vote to determine whether the region will become the next state in the Union. In 2018, a category five storm, Hurricane Maria, hit Puerto Rico with deadly force. It flattened large portions of infrastructure, wiped out all the power and much of the power grid to the entire the island for months, and killed thousands. As a result, many surviving Puerto Ricans sought a new start and moved to the mainland United States.

Another unincorporated territory is the US Virgin Islands, made up of many small islands as well as the large islands of Saint Croix, Saint John, and Saint Thomas. They are in the Caribbean and were purchased from the original occupiers, the Danish, for $25 million in 1917. Today, they are led by an elected governor.

Found in the southern end of the Mariana Islands, Guam is also an unincorporated territory of the United States. The island was added to American holdings during World War I as a way to increase American presence in the Pacific Islands. Though residents of Guam are nonvoting citizens, today the region does participate in American politics though caucuses, and they have a locally elected governor. The Northern Mariana Islands are near Guam.

They were made a part of the United States in 1976 and became a full commonwealth in 1986. This made the islands' people citizens of the United States.

America Samoa is the final US territory in the Pacific Ocean. It is the only region controlled by America where residents are not granted citizenship at birth. To be a citizen, an American Samoan must have a parent who is a citizen or apply for citizenship and be naturalized.

Other American territories outside of American borders include military bases all over the world. More than seventy countries have military bases. In fact, there are about eight hundred United States military bases outside of the United States around the world. Each base is controlled by America and considered a territory of the United States.

America Today

From islands miles away to the rich and frigid Alaskan frontier, the country's borders have expanded far past the imaginations of the Founding Fathers.

The history of the country is stamped on the land through cities and infrastructure, but it is stamped on the world through geopolitical influence. From the early tribes

Grand Teton National Park in Wyoming

who predated the early colonists by thousands of years, to the budding roots of a new nation as seen in the original colonies, to the unique spirit of each state and region that has developed from them, the land shows the exceptional history of the country.

★ CHRONOLOGY ★

★ ★ ★ ★ ★ ★ ★

1492   Christopher Columbus arrives in the Americas, landing in what is now Haiti.

1651   British Parliament passes the Navigation Acts.

1754   The French and Indian War begins.

1773   The Boston Tea Party takes place.

1774   The Coercive Acts are passed.

1776   The American Revolution begins when the Founding Fathers sign the Declaration of Independence.

1783   The Treaty of Paris ends the American Revolution.

1803   The United States acquires the Louisiana Territory through the Louisiana Purchase.

1804   The Lewis and Clark expedition begins on the Ohio River.

1819   The Missouri Compromise goes into effect.

★ ★ ★ ★ ★ ★ ★

1830 President Andrew Jackson passes the Indian
Removal Act.

1849 Gold is found in California.

1854 The Kansas-Nebraska Act is passed, overturning the
ruling of the Missouri Compromise.

1860 Republican Abraham Lincoln is elected president,
sparking the secession of several southern states
from the Union.

1865 General Robert E. Lee surrenders, ending the Civil
War. President Abraham Lincoln is assassinated.
The Thirteenth Amendment is ratified, which
abolishes slavery.

1867 The United States purchases Alaska.

1898 The United States annexes Hawaii.

1906 The National Monuments Act is passed, protecting
historically and scientifically valuable lands.

1929 The Great Depression begins.

1962 The Cuban Missile Crisis takes place 90 miles
(145 km) off the shores of Miami, Florida.

1965 The Water Quality Act is passed.

1967 The Air Quality Act and Clean Air Act are passed.

1973 The United States withdraws from Vietnam.

1992 The Soviet Union dissolves, ending the Cold War.

2010 An explosion on a BP oil rig causes a devastating oil leak in the Gulf of Mexico.

2018 Hurricane Maria hits Puerto Rico.

GLOSSARY

antebellum A descriptor for the era in the mid-1800s leading up to the American Civil War.

battalion A large group of infantry troops ready for battle.

boomtown A town or city that develops very rapidly, usually in response to a sudden economic change or new industry.

cartographer A person who draws and creates maps.

Columbian Exchange The cross-cultural exchange of crops, animals, plants, technology, and disease as a result of European contact with the Americas.

conservation Efforts to preserve, protect, and restore natural resources and wildlife.

containment The United States' efforts to stop the spread of Communism in Europe and the Middle East during the Cold War.

deciduous A forest where the plants and trees lose their leaves every year and regrow them annually.

egalitarian A society in which all people are viewed as equals, both socially and politically.

geopolitical Geographic features that have an impact on politics, especially in foreign relations.

ideology An overarching or communal set of ideas that guide behavior and practices among a group or in a region.

isolationism A national policy to remain separate from international affairs.

Mesoamerica A historical region spanning from Central America to North America that was important during early colonial history.

mujahideen Afghani rebel fighters who protested Soviet presence and later fought under Afghanistan's warlords.

postindustrial society A society that has moved from a manufacturing-based economy into a service-based economy.

Progressives Political and social reformers during the 1920s.

secede To leave a political alliance or union and declare independence.

social stratification The division of communities or countries into different ranks of people.

urbanization The growth of towns or regions into cities; the increased presence of cities in a country.

★ FURTHER INFORMATION ★

★ ★ ★ ★ ★ ★ ★

Books

Field, Paula, Russell Mclean, and Kate Phelps, eds. *The Kingfisher Student Atlas of North America*. Boston: Kingfisher, 2005.

McIlwraith, Thomas F., and Edward K. Muller, eds. *North America: The Historical Geography of a Changing Continent*. Second edition. Lanham, MD: Rowman and Littlefield, 2001.

Spears, Ellen Griffith. *Rethinking the American Environmental Movement Post-1945*. New York: Routledge, 2018.

Websites

Geography & Strategy During the American Revolution

https://sites.google.com/a/email.cpcc.edu/geography-strategy-during-the-american-revolution

Explore the American Revolution through a geographic lens to see how the ill-prepared Continental Army defeated one of the greatest militaries of its era.

★ ★ ★ ★ ★ ★ ★

Historical Maps: North America

https://www.nypl.org/collections/nypl-recommendations/
guides/historical-maps-north-america

The New York Public Library has a wide-ranging digital collection of maps that show the United States' history and the geographic transformation from colonization to present times.

Videos

Crash Course US History #13: Slavery

https://www.youtube.com/watch?v=Ajn9g5Gsv98

Author John Green describes slavery in America and the effect it had on different regions of the United States.

Native American Societies Before Contact

https://www.khanacademy.org/humanities/us-history/
precontact-and-early-colonial-era/before-contact/v/
native-american-societies-before-contact

Watch a short but comprehensive video about Native American societies prior to European contact.

★ BIBLIOGRAPHY ★

Amadeo, Kimberly. "Stock Market Crash of 1929 Facts, Causes, and Impact." *The Balance*. Last modified April 5, 2018. https://www.thebalance.com/stock-market-crash-of-1929-causes-effects-and-facts-3305891.

Department of State Office of the Historian. "The Annexation of Texas, the Mexican-American War, and the Treaty of Guadalupe-Hidalgo, 1845, 1848." Retrieved June 6, 2018. https://history.state.gov/milestones/1830-1860/texas-annexation.

———. "Louisiana Purchase, 1803." Retrieved June 6, 2018. https://history.state.gov/milestones/1801-1829/louisiana-purchase.

George Washington's Mount Vernon. "Valley Forge." 2018. https://www.mountvernon.org/library/digitalhistory/digital-encyclopedia/article/valley-forge.

The Gilder Lehrman Institute of American History. "Columbus Reports on His First Voyage, 1493." 2017. https://www.gilderlehrman.org/content/columbus-reports-his-first-voyage-1493.

———. "Paul Revere's Engraving of the Boston Massacre, 1770." 2017. https://www.gilderlehrman.org/content/ paul-revere%E2%80%99s-engraving-boston- massacre-1770.

Hayes, Derek. *Historical Atlas of the United States.* Los Angeles: University of California Press, 2007.

The History Place. "The Kansas-Nebraska Act." 1996. http:// www.historyplace.com/lincoln/kansas.htm.

Kuepper, Justin. "3 Of The Most Lucrative Land Deals in History." Investopedia, August 23, 2017. https://www. investopedia.com/financial-edge/1012/3-of-the-most- lucrative-land-deals-in-history.aspx.

Legal Information Institute. "Plessy v. Ferguson." Retrieved June 8, 2018. https://www.law.cornell.edu/ supremecourt/text/163/537.

Lewis & Clark's Historic Trail. "Journals." 2018. https:// lewisclark.net/journals.

Library of Congress. "Indian Removal Act." Retrieved June 6, 2018. https://www.loc.gov/rr/program/bib/ourdocs/ indian.html.

Massachusetts Historical Society. "Henry Pelham." Last
modified 2018. http://www.masshist.org/terrafirma/
pelham.

National Park Service. "Historic Tribes of the Great Basin."
Last modified February 28, 2015. https://www.nps.gov/
grba/learn/historyculture/historic-tribes-of-the-great-
basin.htm.

NSA CSS. "Indications of Soviet Arms Shipment to Cuba,
Weekly COMINT Economic Briefing." Last modified
May 3, 2016. https://www.nsa.gov/news-features/
declassified-documents/cuban-missile-crisis.

Nunn, Nathan, and Nancy Qian. "The Columbian Exchange:
A History of Disease, Food, and Ideas." *The Journal of
Economic Perspectives* 24, no. 2 (Spring 2010): 163-188.

Prine Pauls, Elizabeth. "Northwest Coast Indian."
Encyclopedia Britannica. Last modified September 22,
2017. https://www.britannica.com/topic/Northwest-
Coast-Indian.

Schamotta, Justin. "Ways That Geography Affected the
American Revolution." *Classroom.* Last modified May 14,
2018. https://classroom.synonym.com/ways-geography-
affected-american-revolution-8414372.html.

Schimmer, Russell. "Hispaniola." Yale Genocide Studies Program. 2018. https://gsp.yale.edu/case-studies/colonial-genocides-project/hispaniola.

Woolner, David B. "FDR and the New Deal Response to an Environmental Catastrophe." *Roosevelt Institute.* Last modified June 6, 2010. http://rooseveltinstitute.org/fdr-and-new-deal-response-environmental-catastrophe.

★ INDEX ★

egalitarian, 13
environmentalism, 64, 66,
  76, 88, 90
European colonization,
  15–21
exports, 21, 24, 84

formal warfare, 29
Fourteenth Amendment,
  57, 60
French colonization, 19–20,
  22, 32

genocide, 16, 18
geopolitical, 28, 96
global warming, 89–90
gold, 15–16, 19, 44–45
Grand Canyon, **4**, 5
Great Basin, 10, 46
Great Depression, 70, 72, 76
greenhouse gases, 88-90, **91**
guerrilla warfare, 29

Hawaii, 89, 94–95
Hoover, President Herbert,
  69, 72-74

ideology, 24, 44, 50, 64, 81

industrialization, 50, 52–53,
  59, 62–64, 88
Industrial Revolution, 33, 62
isolationism, 86

Jefferson, Thomas, 37–39
Jim Crow laws, 58

Korean and Vietnamese
  Wars, 82-84, **83**, 88

Lewis, Meriwether, **36**, 39
Lincoln, Abraham, 53, 57, 89
longhouse, **7**, 8
Louisiana Purchase, 37, **38**,
  39, 42

Manifest Destiny, 44, 89
Mesoamerica, 17, 19
Mexican-American War, 44
Missouri Compromise, 42, 52
mujahideen, 86

national parks, 65–66, **65**,
  89, **97**
Native Americans, 6–7, 9–10,
  13, 15–16, 18, 20, 22, 25,
  29, 34, 39, 45, 48

★ ABOUT THE AUTHOR ★

★ ★ ★ ★ ★ ★ ★

Cassandra Schumacher has a background in anthropology and creative writing with a focus in cultural and historical studies. She is the author of numerous books for high school students, including *Discovering America: Work, Exchange, and Technology in the United States*. Schumacher's interests are vast and varied but predominantly focus on the study of human and cultural identity throughout history into modern times. Much of her writing focuses on sociocultural interactions and power dynamics.

★ ★ ★ ★ ★ ★ ★